BUILDING WEALTH DURING RECESSION

Discover How To Make Money During Economic Depression

CHRISTOPHER HOLMES

CONTENTS

CHAPTER 1

For companies, the time of recessions may be very challenging. Economic recessions are times of economic contraction that halt an economy's organic development, increase unemployment, and often compel business organisations to downsize or even shut down. They might be mild lulls in an otherwise robust development cycle or more severe, protracted downturns. Economists monitor a wide range of economic indicators to spot various categories of recessions and their corresponding recoveries. Depending on the variables that form a recession, it is in turn determined by how much economic activity declines, the impact on the economy and how long that decline lasts, a recession may fall into more than one category at once.

Understanding the similarities and distinctions among the many sorts of recessions will be essential for any firm striving to thrive — or even just survive — during the downturn, regardless of the type of recession an economy is experiencing.

Types of Recession

The way that recessions change an economy's trajectory of economic growth defines them. Since the major method by which economists categorize recessions is by the form their recoveries take, a recession's final kind may not be obvious from its outset. The graphs that appear when the gross domestic product (GDP) is plotted through time, from the start of the recession to its recovery, are designated V, U, W, L, and K, and they represent some of the most typical forms of recession recoveries. When examined more closely, recessions often fit into more than one category, depending on the sector or how various enterprises or demographic groups are impacted, for example. For instance, some industries were able to transition to remote work and function nearly normally following the COVID-19 economic shutdown in 2020, which resulted in a recession whose official timing extended from February to April of that year (the shortest on record). This resulted in a V-shaped recovery. However, others that couldn't, like the live entertainment industry, recovered considerably more slowly. As a result, the final form of that recession may resemble a K, with various businesses turning around at various dates and rebounding at various rates.

Short-term downturns may be followed by an expansionary phase that "catch up" to prior expectations and puts the economy back on track. For instance, the U.S. recession from 1973 to 1975 matches the bill. Not all recessions, however, are brief; some have a lasting impact on the economy's upward trajectory. The effects of the 2008 financial crisis are still being felt in many nations, including the U.K., whose economies are still less than they would have been otherwise.

Main Points

- **An economy shrinks during a recession, which is often accompanied by growing unemployment**

and negative growth in GDP and income.

- **Recessions are mostly classed based on how they recover. Different economic sectors may be impacted quite differently during recessions since they are not all the same.**
- **Recessions sometimes have reasons that are related to them, such as a rise in interest rates, a significant shift in consumer confidence and spending patterns, or interruptions in supply networks.**
- **Until one ends, the complete picture of a recession is often obscure.**

Why do Recessions Occur?

A contemporary economy's production often increases with time. But that doesn't imply that its growth is always linear. In general, economies go through peaks and valleys, booms and busts, like a wave inclined upward or a Slinky climbing a flight of stairs (if such a Slinky were possible). A recession is characterized as a trough that lasts long enough to affect an economy's overall growth. Recessions may continue for years or only a few months. There are several methods for identifying a recession, some of which are based on average unemployment rates and others which take fluctuations in GDP into account. The National Bureau of Economic Research (NEBR), a U.S. agency that "calls" recessions, examines a broad range of economic data to identify the "three Ds" of a recession: "depth, diffusion, and duration."

The relative importance of each of the "Ds" may change

depending on the kind of recession. For instance, the COVID-19 epidemic resulted in a significant decline that spread to all areas of the economy, although it did not take long, economically speaking, before certain markets began to rebound. However, neither has that recovery been straightforward or linear; rather, it varies widely depending on the causes or industries you consider. If the supply is soon restored, other recessions, such as those brought on by a sudden supply shock, may also be brief. Or, if the supply cannot be recovered, they can compel an economy to choose a different course.

On the consumer's involvement during a recession, many economists concentrate. Consumers may start conserving more and cutting down on their spending if they lose faith in the economy. Businesses may be forced to cut down on expenditure when less money is spent on products and services. This may include decreasing pay and reducing worker size, which would increase unemployment and weaken consumer spending power and prolong the downturn in the economic cycle. The same can be said for ineffective spending habits: If people or firms cease using their money wisely, they may wind up taking on more debt than they can manage or expanding into areas that their business model cannot sustain should the economy's development halt. This results in bloated enterprises that es may result in defaults on debt and company failures, and, if prevalent enough, might affect the economy.

Although many of the recessions covered here have some of the same indications, traits, and causes, no two recessions are identical. Realistically, there is no one perfect explanation for why a recession occurs or doesn't. The large structures that makeup economies continually fluctuate in a variety of ways, causing ripple effects that may spread out locally or far. They can only really make a difference when they expand and come together. This is mentioned by economist Irving Fisher, who claims that because there are "innumerable variables" in economic systems, assuming that one or a small number of reasons caused a recession typically results in an incomplete picture.

CHAPTER 2

Different Types of Recessions

Recessions can be brought on by a wide range of interconnected factors, many of which have predictable patterns like the booms and busts of the business cycle. A business leader can better understand what is causing a recession and how to weather it or take advantage of opportunities by being aware of some common recession types.

The Boom-Bust Recession

Like a rope wound around a stairway railing, most economies have ups and downs while their overall growth improves. An economy that "booms," or expands faster than expected over the long term, frequently experience inflation. A central bank or other government supervisory body often implements measures to "cool" the economy and avoid overheating to manage inflation. Typically, these measures involve raising taxes, lowering government spending, or increasing interest rates. This may result in lower overall consumer spending and a shift in consumers' priorities toward debt repayment and savings, which may lead to a recession or "bust." The U.K.'s 1990–1992 recession was a collapse that came after a late 1980s boom.

Financial Recession

A recession with a negative balance of payments often occurs when an economy has too much debt. In typical times, financial institutions lend out the money that individuals and corporations save with them to other people and companies, keeping the economy humming. When consumer and company spending patterns change as a result of worries about debt levels, everyone starts to cut down on spending at the same time to "clean up their balance sheets." Increases in government spending or reduced taxes may continue to encourage borrowers to pay down large debts rather than spend, making it difficult to exit a balance sheet recession. If everyone is saving, less money is going into growth, which might lengthen the recessionary phase, similar to what occurs when a decline in consumer confidence causes consumers to reassess their priorities.

Slow growth plagued Japan's economy for decades after the recession began as firms continued to pay off loans even when interest rates dropped as low as 0% during the "Lost Decades" recession of the 1990s, which followed the fall of its real estate boom. Japan's GDP growth over the long run has never completely recovered from that downturn.

Depression

A recession could be upgraded to depression if it persists for years or decades. Recessions and depressions often have the same traits, although depression is more severe. The economy may experience GDP losses of over 10%, unemployment rates near to or over 30%, and a significant reorganization; most depressions result in slower growth over a prolonged period. Many of the rules put in place during the Great Depression of the

1930s—including the New Deal—restructured how the economy operated at the time.

Availability Shock

Global occurrences, such as wars, natural catastrophes, or public health crises, may significantly disrupt local or global supply networks and send an economy into recession. For instance, when oil prices spiked in the 1970s, companies and consumers were compelled to spend more on oil-based goods, such as gasoline, which left them with less money to spend elsewhere, triggering a recession. These recessions may not endure for very long if the supply is immediately restored. But if not, the impacts of the supply shock might last for years, as is the case with the ongoing supply problems brought on by the COVID-19 epidemic. They may also result in a long-term movement toward supply chain diversification or changing how products are utilized, such as an increase in investments in alternative fuels like natural gas or solar energy as a result of an oil crisis.

Different Recession Recovery Methods

Recessions cannot be completely understood or categorized until they have passed, and often not even then when the next recession has started and the entire image of the preceding recession is seen. Imagine someone penning a note: Before the pen lifts off the paper and starts the following letter, it's impossible to know whether a letter is a V or merely the beginning part of a W.

Recession in a V-shape

Even after a sharp decline, V-shaped recessions don't endure as long as other types of recessions, and they often have the least lasting effects on GDP growth in general. Following a short-term interruption, such as a resolvable supply chain issue or a seasonal change for an area, growth often resumes its prior tendencies. An increase in interest rates to prevent inflation following the Korean War, as was predicted, contributed to the U.S. recession of 1953. Less than a year later, demand returned because financial reserves were made accessible and interest rates were lowered when inflation was not as high as anticipated. A V-shaped recovery is characterized by a rapid return to the economy's pre-recession growth trajectory.

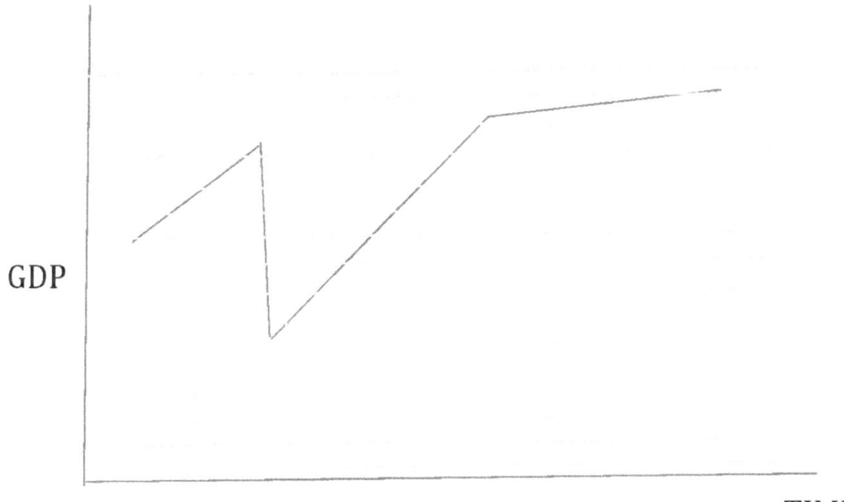

U-Shaped Recession in a V-Shape

When compared to a V-shaped depression, a U-shaped recession experiences a lengthier period of decline and/or stagnation before returning to its prior growth path. Even if there is some temporary recovery, the GDP curve's trough lasts longer than in a V-shaped recession before finally rising to the initial growth projections. The US had a U-shaped recession in 1973, and it took until 1976 for GDP to reach its pre-recession high.

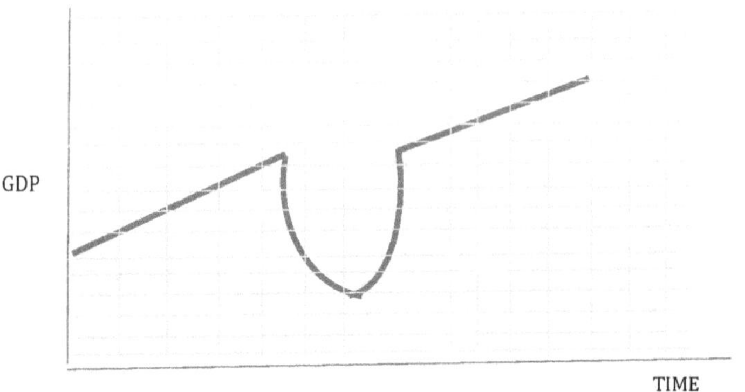

Recession in a W-Shape

A W-shaped recession has a second drop following the start of a recovery. These may have a more significant effect on consumer confidence since the second decline makes many people wait longer than they would have otherwise before beginning to spend money again out of concern about a further decline in the future. W-shaped recessions, despite how the letter W appears, don't usually resemble two Vs. For instance, the American economy had a brief V-shaped drop in the early 1980s before quickly rebounding. However, the second drop that completed the W in 1981 lasted more than a year and, on its own, seemed to be closer to a U.

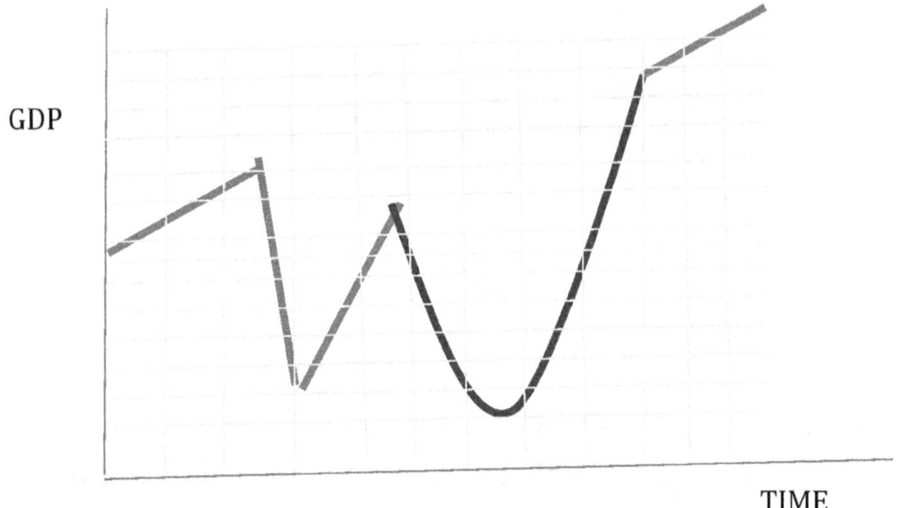

L-Shaped Recession with a W-Shape

The most worrisome recession patterns are L-shaped ones: They have long-term effects on growth, permanently slowing GDP's rate of growth and often bringing it close to depressive levels. The economy is just slowly recovering, unemployment is still high, and investments are still low. Given that GDP growth was regularly less than 2% and often negative for more than a decade, Greece's 2008 recession is seen as an L-shaped recession or depression.

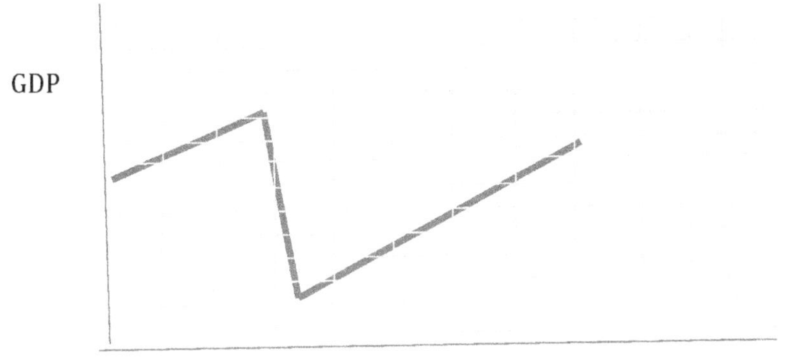

Recession in a K-Shape

Different economic sectors have seen recoveries during a K-shaped recession. A V- or U-shaped recovery may occur for one group, whereas a slower recovery or a longer period of negative development may occur for another. The groupings might be divided based on the groups' industries, classes, generations, or demographics. Often, rather than drawing new divisions between the groups, the economic recovery just accentuates existing ones. Many believe that the recovery from the COVID-19-related recession that lasted from February to April 2020 took the form of a K shape because the stock market and other industries that benefit from remote work recovered much more quickly than many others, such as in-person dining and live entertainment.

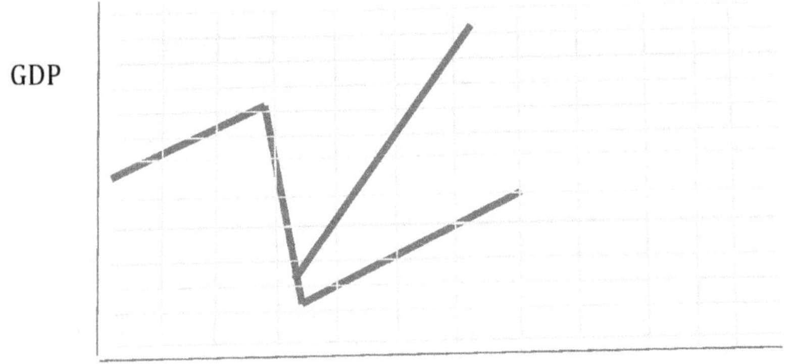

Recession with a normal square root

The graphed curve of a typical square root recession resembles the mathematical "radical" sign used to represent a number's square root. Due to a prolonged period of expansion, the recovery ends up being greater than the original, but it does not maintain this tendency and instead temporarily flattens out. The increase is often stopped during the flattening phase by an external cause, such as a supply limitation.

Recession with an inverted or reverse square root of the norm

Reverse square root recessions also have curves that resemble radical symbols, but are inverted and seem to be mirror images of them. This recession has a V-shaped initial collapse and rapid recovery, but it then encounters a roadblock and plateaus. Some countries have been suffering from a reverse square root recession since the 2020 recession as they partly reopen their economy but maintain some pandemic restrictions, impeding a complete return to pre-crisis levels.

square root inverted in reverse

Reevaluating your company's effectiveness during a recession may be the best course of action. A business that wants to emerge from the recession stronger than ever may find that cutting costs and reducing spending on less lucrative activities is beneficial. An excellent moment to diversify a company model is during a recession, particularly if it involves a market that is less impacted by the recessionary economic patterns. Many eateries increased their delivery options during the COVID-19 epidemic or provided new goods to replace the services they were unable to provide while closed. Other businesses used hybrid models or remote work policies that reduced office expenditures while boosting productivity and employee loyalty. A firm may traverse the risks of a recession with the use of contingency planning.

The form, length, and subsequent recoveries of recessions may be influenced by a wide range of various factors. These factors might include supply or economic shocks, natural catastrophes, or public health emergencies. A firm may better prepare for a specific recession by understanding the similarities and differences between the many kinds of recessions and their recoveries. These variables may include consumer confidence, interest rates, pricing, and supply chain problems. These insights may aid in a business's readiness for recovery, regardless of its form.

FAQs about Recession Types

What are the top 5 causes of recession?

There are many reasons why recessions occur, but there are five that stand out:

- Natural disasters
- Public health crises
- International unrest like wars
- Disruptive technological change
- A sharp increase in the price of oil or other commodities
- Significant changes in consumer confidence and spending patterns.

The Five Stages Of Recession

Real income reduction, growing unemployment, a drop in industrial production, a drop in sales, and a drop in monthly GDP are the five primary signs of a recession.

What distinguishes a recession from a depression?

An economic slump that is more severe than a recession is called depression. Although they have many similarities, a recession becomes a depression when the GDP declines by more than 10%, there are many company failures, and the unemployment rate is at or above 30%. Recessions are also shorter than depressions, which often endure for several years and force an economic reorganization.

The different types of recession

Recessions today include the 2020 slump brought on by the COVID-19 pandemic shutdowns, the 2008 financial crisis (commonly referred to as the Great Recession), and the early 1980s downturn that followed an interruption in the world's oil supply in 1979.

A U-shaped recession

An economic slump that finally resumes the previous growth path is known as a U-shaped recession, but only after a protracted period of stagnant or weak growth. Recovery in a U shape often takes many years.

IMPACT OF RECESSION ON BUSINESSES

Business executives who don't know what to anticipate dread the phrase "recession." However, strength comes from knowledge. This chapter looks at how a recession may appear and how it might affect your company when the inevitable next one comes around.

What Effect Do Recessions Have on Business?

Economic studies indicate that although the majority of firms suffer during recessions, a sizeable minority emerge undamaged or even stronger. According to conventional knowledge, larger is better when it comes to firm size and industry, there is a correlation between these qualities and how well a corporation does during a recession. However, there are no assurances. A small firm that is prepared might do better than an unprepared giant corporation. Additionally, private enterprises often have a little bit more financial latitude than publicly traded corporations, which are under pressure to fulfil quarterly profit targets.

However, companies that prosper and survive a recession often have two things in common: cash on hand and access to finance. Both are typical problems for small and midsize companies in normal times, which is why it's so important to "recession-proof" your company well in advance of the inevitable next downturn.

Main Points

- **Periods of diminishing economic activity known as recessions sometimes occur as a result of the regular business cycle.**
- **Recessions hurt the majority of firms, while preparedness may lessen the damage.**
- **Recessionary corporate activity such as lower profitability, job losses, tighter lending, and operational adjustments are all sparked by declining consumer spending.**
- **Recessions may provide chances for organizations that are in good positions if they are supported by the appropriate financial systems and strategies.**

CHAPTER 3

Impact of Recession on Business

The effects of a recession spread to other areas of the economy. Businesses often scale down operations when consumer demand for goods and services declines. This results in a reduction in the need for labour and resources, which in turn lowers business-to-business expenditure. Therefore, unemployment rises, further decreasing consumer demand. It's crucial to remember that firms and individuals continue to spend throughout a recession, but at lower rates and with different objectives.

A recession's domino effects have a variety of repercussions on firms, including:

Decreased profits: Consumer confidence in the economy decreases before and during a recession, and consumers make fewer purchases. Companies whose breakeven threshold is greater than the present demand may experience substantial pressure on sales and profit as a result of this softening or outright decline in demand. When sales decline and costs stay the same, profits decline or disappear completely. Every company can survive a time of decreased profits or losses, but the longer the recession lasts, the greater the likelihood that it will cause problems.

Business owners find it challenging to reinvest during a recession due to lower profitability, which has a lasting impact long when the economy starts to recover. For instance, if consumers are reducing their discretionary spending, a restaurant that is staffed to handle a particular number of tables each night would probably notice a reduction in revenues if only half of those tables are full. Due to this, the owner could put off getting new kitchen equipment, which might put the restaurant behind when it comes to growth.

Tighter credit requirements: When determining a borrower's creditworthiness during a recession, lenders often use stricter standards. This may prevent some small enterprises from getting the crucial cash they need. Meanwhile, tighter credit restrictions may lead to higher borrowing prices. Consumers may see decreases in personal credit or higher interest rates, which may lead them to cut down on spending or put off purchases, which, of course, exacerbates a company's demand-side issues. Take into account a furniture shop that finances its inventory acquisitions with a revolving credit line. The number of goods the furniture business may buy and subsequently sell to its clients may be restricted by a decrease in the amount of available credit or total cancellation of the credit line. Lost sales result from low supply levels or stockouts. Relatedly, financially stressed homeowners may not be able to purchase furniture on credit, leading them to forego or postpone buying.

Decrease in cash flow: For many companies, getting cash in the door is a constant problem, but it may become much more challenging during a recession. Due to their cash flow problems, customers can take longer to pay, which might result in a higher proportion of accounts receivable that are uncollectible. As a result, companies can find themselves unable to pay their suppliers and workers on time. Businesses may be obliged to use their cash reserves, make just minimal debt payments, and extend payment periods as long as they can as a result of limited credit lines. For instance, a restaurant owner can delay paying food suppliers while still buying food to keep his business operating. The incoming cash flow of the food providers, therefore, decreases as well.

Declining stock prices and dividends: Not only small and medium firms are affected by a recession. The same revenue issues affect publicly traded corporations, which might result in lower-than-expected profit results and a decrease in stock prices. Because capital markets are a substantial source of financing for publicly traded corporations, this is a concern. Additionally, dividend distributions could be lower than expected when earnings are squeezed. This may result in discontent among shareholders, damage to the management team's image, and a possible decline in stock prices.

Decline in Product quality; Business owners may opt to skimp on raw materials in an attempt to save costs and boost profitability in the face of dwindling sales. Customers also interpret shrinkflation, when a firm sells fewer goods for the same price, as a drop in quality. These strategies could boost profits in the near term, but they might backfire over time. When times are tough, consumers value quality and durability more, and a noticeable drop in quality might lead to further declines in demand. For instance, customers may choose less costly store brands if the value proposition for something as essential as disposable newborn diapers declines.

Cutbacks in benefits or employee layoffs. The national unemployment rate increased from 5% to 9.5% during the recession of 2008. Indeed, when profits fall and cash flow slows, businesses frequently reduce benefits or lay off employees. Small firms are often the first to fire workers during a downturn and the first to hire them back when the economy starts to recover. Companies cut labour expenses during recessions in additional ways than only via layoffs. Some people decide to stop all new hiring and leave all available posts unfilled. Some continue to employ people but cut down on work hours. And yet others could decide to cut down on employee perks, such as eliminating 401(k) matching or making workers pay a higher share of health-plan expenses. Of course, when company activity drops, strategic, proportionate workforce cutbacks or furloughs may be required.

Reduced demand: According to a study by the Federal Reserve Bank of New York, the main factor contributing to businesses' difficulties during recessions is a decline in customer demand for their goods and services. Even while it may seem apparent, it is the most uncontrolled issue that company owners must deal with. Ironically, company owners often reduce marketing and promotion spending during a recession, even though this is the time when they should be cultivating client loyalty and capturing market share from failing firms. Consider the situation of food providers who are experiencing a reduced cash flow. Giving regular clients a discount for early payment might be one way to maintain demand. By doing this, the food provider may be able to maintain its clientele, collect money faster, and maybe boost sales from existing clients once the recovery gets going.

Operational adjustments: Businesses are often forced to make do with less during recessions, which frequently forces them to reconsider how they do business. Operational improvements include anything from streamlining procedures and workflows to automating repetitive tasks and beyond to enhance productivity, lower expenses overall, and raise profitability. Small enterprises often have more operational flexibility than their bigger competitors. If demand for fine dining falls to an untenable level, our restaurant's owner, for instance, may decide to supply meal kits.

Restrictions on marketing.: During a recession, businesses that resist the need to completely cut marketing expenditures often set spending constraints. These limitations show themselves in the strategies used and the emphasis. Aligning the "4Ps" of the marketing mix — product, pricing, placement, and promotion — with changes in customer behaviour that are often seen during recessions, such as a greater focus on quality and durability, is a difficulty. Redirecting efforts connected to product placement or distribution toward deepening client penetration is one example of a common change in emphasis brought on by marketing limitations since doing so is often less expensive than attracting new consumers. The recession's effect on marketing strategies is a move away from costly media buys and toward low-cost "guerilla marketing."

Price war: When recessionary sales start to slacken, price reductions to maintain market share are a usual response. However, this can start a price war amongst rivals, further reducing profitability. Customers whose price sensitivity is increased during recessions might profit from price wars, but it is difficult for businesses that lack significant financial reserves to weather the unknowable length of time before growth resumes. Price wars may also hinder a company's capacity to resume regular pricing when demand increases. Producer prices dropped by 8% during the Great Recession, and it took over two years for them to recover.

Advantages Of Recession for businesses

Recessions aren't always terrible for companies, and some even profit from them despite their difficulties. Healthcare, food and beverage, utilities, and other so-called "defensive" businesses are examples of industries that are inherently more recession-proof than others because consumers consider their goods necessary regardless of economic situations. The difficulties brought on by a recession, however, may spur inventive thinking that eventually enhances enterprises in other sectors, making them more effective, innovative, financially responsible, and/or profitable when the economy recovers. Businesses that fail may also offer certain assets at deep discounts to companies. A recession offers two advantages economically:

A straightforward definition of inflation is the pace at which the cost of everyday products rises while the economy is doing well. When there is a lot of demand, vendors raise their pricing. However, inflation often decreases during a recession as demand drops and sellers are more inclined to reduce prices to shift inventory. Prices will drop, which will be advantageous to companies and those with cash or credit to spend.

Low-interest rates: To reduce the speed of the impending recession, the Federal Open Market Committee (FOMC), which determines the "policy" interest rates for the U.S. central bank, lowers its rates at the first signs of a downturn. In response, lenders reduce their interest rates on consumer loans like credit cards, mortgages, and vehicle loans, as well as commercial loans and lines of credit. The idea is that reduced borrowing costs would encourage expenditure, which will maintain economic growth. A recession may indirectly cut loan payments for companies that meet the tougher lending requirements set by lenders for low-interest borrowing.

Cycle-based recessions often have a detrimental effect on a lot of firms. Reduced client demand results in revenue issues, which have an impact on both the business's operations and the economy as a whole.

Business leaders may better prepare and put plans in place to lessen the effects the next time one occurs by being aware of the possible effects of a recession.

FAQs on Impact of Recession

How are recessions different for small firms vs big enterprises?

Reduced profitability brought on by diminishing client demand might worsen enduring problems for small businesses including cash flow and credit availability. But during a recession, a well-positioned small firm may do better than a big, unprepared one.

What effects does a recession have?

For both consumers and companies, recessions set off a series of related events. Businesses operate more slowly when consumers start making fewer purchases. They need fewer labour and resources, which might lead to job losses and poor commercial demand, both of which would further reduce consumer demand. Reduced profitability, slower cash flow, and falling stock prices are just a few effects that may harm businesses.

Which industries experience a recession?

During a recession, the majority of firms experience losses. Travel and tourism, leisure cars, personal services, conferences, and fine dining are some examples of "nonessential" businesses that are often hurt harder by recessions than "defensive" industries. This is because demand for their goods—such as those related to healthcare, utilities, necessities, and food and drink—remains steady regardless of macroeconomic circumstances.

CHAPTER 4

Businesses that can weather a recession

While no firm is fully immune to a downturn, many are recession-resistant sectors and business strategies, doing well even while other businesses are cutting expenses and battling to survive. The fact that certain commodities and services, like food and healthcare, are requirements is one of the factors that contribute to this problem. Additionally, consumers are impacted by a recession in a variety of ways: Some scarcely alter their spending patterns, while others just spend what is necessary. Small indulgences still fit within most people's budgets.

Even if your company is not yet recession-proof, you can start preparing or making changes now to make the most of difficult times.

What Are Business Models That Are Recession-Proof?

When other company types may be compelled to cut expenses, downsize their workforces, or even shut down, a recession-proof firm or business strategy continues to operate effectively. These countercyclical enterprises either fulfil customer needs even in times of economic distress or see a rise in demand for their goods or services.

Main Points

- **Despite the economic downturn, consumers continue to purchase essentials, but they may**

select less costly choices and fewer amounts.

- **People who are untouched by economic instability will continue to spend money on luxury brands and pricier essentials that they think will last longer.**
- **Pet maintenance has become a necessary expense for both younger and older generations ready to spend on their "fur babies," alongside healthcare and childcare.**

Recession-Proof Companies

A company requires strong leadership, a great product or service, attentive customer care, and an understanding of industry trends to survive a recession. However, owing to the nature of their products and the way customers change their purchasing habits in their favour during hard times, certain company types are better positioned to withstand adverse economic situations than others.

Suggested Recession-Proof Business Models

Food and creature comfort service

Families and companies alike avoid luxury products like vacations, corporate events, fine dining, and pricey catered lunches during recessions. Food is still a need, however, and cheap creature pleasures might seem like a luxury at a lower price. Additionally, when things are rough financially, many people may feel like they need to escape with food and booze.

Candy sales: During the 2019 pandemic, candy sales, a less costly creature comfort, skyrocketed. "Sugar cheers up many people whose spirits have been lowered by the weak economy. For others, candy serves as a sentimental reminiscence of happier times. Not to mention, it is reasonably priced. Although many people may see a premium confection as a luxury, the price point allows more consumers to "splurge" on a sweet delicacy and may do so more often than with more costly pleasures.

Grocery businesses: While restaurants may see a decline in dine-in business during a recession, convenience stores and other inexpensive grocery stores often experience growth as people search for easy methods to pick up essentials. During the brief COVID-19 recession, 41% of UK consumers started shopping at smaller neighbourhood stores instead of bigger supermarkets. They not only seek neighbouring stores, but they also purchase food in lesser amounts. During recessions, consumers are often motivated to support small, neighbourhood companies.

Food delivery services: During the COVID-19 pandemic lockdown, purchases of another tiny indulgence—orders to food delivery services—rose. Meal delivery services like Blue Apron or Gobble offered customers who were stranded at home but didn't love cooking a compromise between eating at restaurants and doing their meal planning and preparation. As more people switched to working and going to school from home, the usage of app-based takeout and delivery ordering services surged among those who could afford restaurant alternatives. The recent recession gave these food delivery businesses such a boost that DoorDash filed for its IPO in December 2020 and Instacart raised more than $200 million at roughly the same time.

Vending machines: Similar to confectionery shops, vending machine companies thrive during economic downturns. They often provide everyday basics like food and drinks on the road in addition to a cheap delight. Benefits for company owners include the flexibility to relocate the vending machine to regions with better traffic if sales decline in the initial location.

Alcohol: According to research, usage of alcohol is rising as employment declines. Beer sales decreased during the Great Recession, while sales of spirits rose significantly in contrast. Alcohol retailers that shifted to online sales and delivery saw an increase during the most recent recession. Throughout the pandemic, there was a change in the demand for alcohol as well: "When Covid-19 initially struck, there was a tendency toward value in quantity, "but then, around halfway through, [people] discovered they had more free time because they weren't commuting or going out to bars and restaurants anymore."

Fast food: Vices often rank among the industries that are most resilient to economic downturns. During the Great Recession and the COVID-19 epidemic, however, a lot of individuals also went to coffee shops and other quick-service eateries that offered free WiFi. Consumers believed they had paid their dues for using the internet to find employment, create their websites, and commute to work for the cost of a sandwich or breakfast.

Medications and home care

Even when the economy is weak, healthcare cannot cease. For seniors and older folks, who often still have discretionary money during a recession because they're already out of the employment market, it's particularly crucial. As a result, business models for medical practices, in-home care, medicines, and elder housing are recession-proof.

In-home care is often one of the final things that families choose to discontinue since the services provided by in-home care or home healthcare are frequently not patients' choices. There isn't a less costly option since family members often cannot provide the specialized care that in-home nurses or assistants can. Additionally, if a doctor prescribes home health care, Medicare will also pay for it.

Senior living: The population is becoming older, regardless of the economy. Senior living facilities are the next level of care as more people get to the point where their children or in-home caregivers can no longer handle their demands. According to data, persons 65 and older are protected from recessions since they often own their houses entirely or don't own them anymore and rely on Social Security and pensions that are unaffected by changes in the economy. Because their target market is less impacted by a recession, senior care facilities—whether partial or full service—weather economic shifts effectively.

Pharmaceuticals: People still require their drugs during a recession, just as they do with other aspects of healthcare. Even though a large portion of American healthcare is provided by employers, those who need particular prescriptions will continue to need them whether or not the cost of their life-saving medications goes up or down. The main threats to pharmaceutical companies during economic downturns are legislative changes brought on by the recession.

Pet care

According to research, as more millennials choose not to get married or have children, they are adopting animals at a faster rate to make up for the companionship they are losing. "Millennials make up 25% of the country's population, but they own 35% of all pets, making them the pet ownership generation with the highest percentage in the United States, In addition, older generations are adopting dogs for companionship, and they often have more money available for such purchases.

Veterinarians: In a downturn, pet healthcare is just as important as human healthcare. From 1991 to 2015, the total amount spent on pet care climbed substantially. This period encompassed two recessions. Americans are more inclined to keep pets. Spending on pets has increased. In fact, during a recession, we spend more money on our dogs.

Pet grooming: Depending on the kind of pet a person has, grooming is an additional approach to maintain the health of their furry family members. Some animals need regular, professional grooming to avoid uncomfortable hair and nail overgrowths, maintain joint and dental health, and spot early illness symptoms. However, DIY grooming means more people are buying shampoos, electric shavers, brushes, nail trimmers, and other pet grooming equipment during a recession because they want to save money.

Pet necessities: While budget-conscious consumers may forego upscale meals and other frills for themselves, they often do not do so for their dogs. During the most recent recession, e-commerce alternatives for purchasing and delivering pet food also increased, allowing pet owners to have their chosen brands and food varieties delivered right to their homes. According to Packaged Facts consumer research on pet food in the U.S., "Although the pandemic is far from over, and its economic fallout is likely to linger for many months, if not years, the pet food market is expected to maintain strong growth, bolstered by the infusion of new pets and U.S. pet owners' willingness to spend on their beloved "fur babies" even amid a health and economic crisis."

Home and commercial services

Because individuals consider routine, continuing maintenance to be a prudent investment, the home and business services industry does well throughout recessions. By making smaller repairs and performing routine maintenance, customers and businesses can avoid major malfunctions and, consequently, major expenses. Making a large purchase now, when suppliers are scrambling for customers, may make sense if it will result in better long-term savings, such as in the case of a more energy-efficient HVAC system. However, in the interim, make small fixes work until finances are in a better position.

HVAC and plumbing are two areas where people and companies alike look to cut costs when a recession hits. In addition to being necessities for many, plumbing, heating, and air conditioning are also services that people are looking for the best deals on during economic downturns. To save energy and water and lower utility costs during the Great Recession, several companies made investments in newer, more efficient HVAC and plumbing systems. To prevent the larger costs of replacement or considerable repair, people look into water-saving toilets and faucets and maintain their HVAC systems gradually during recessions.

Automobile repair: During a recession, consumers want to avoid the significant expense of a new car, just like they do with home repairs. They can set aside money for minor repairs and upkeep by giving their cars routine maintenance. While the COVID-19 recession prompted many individuals to work from home and use their automobiles less, the lockdowns delayed the manufacturing of new vehicles, increasing the value of existing cars. As such, frequent automobile maintenance was vital in avoiding the price of a car loan but also the inability to go about if required auto repairs weren't completed.

Utilities: The demand for power, water, natural gas,

and garbage services stays constant despite the financial shifts that occur during a recession. Even in difficult economic times, utility services often provide steady income. Although consumers may discover techniques to reduce their consumption, it is sometimes impossible to stop it.

When it comes to business, corporations prefer to maintain what they already have rather than incur the expenditure of purchasing new equipment. The service may be already planned for or even paid for since many businesses already have maintenance plans in place for their most costly pieces of equipment. For this reason, companies that specialize in equipment and technology repair and routine maintenance may survive a recession effectively.

Goods and services for kids

Being a parent never ceases, even if other aspects of life could be put on hold during a recession. Regardless of the nation's financial status, demand for baby items and other services linked to children continues to be high and often necessary. Diapers, childcare, and education are needs, but parents may be able to sacrifice some of their budget for "nice-to-haves."

Baby items: Before cutting down on baby supplies, parents would often trim other costs. Even while extravagant birthday celebrations may be postponed, newborns and toddlers still need formula, baby food, bottles, and diapers. Kids will constantly need clothing in the following size up as they continue to grow. While there are methods to save expenses, like using cloth diapers, secondhand clothing, or making your baby food, the money you save is often spent on other things, like washing and organic foods.

Childcare services: The COVID-19 recession brought to light the necessity for daycare to support the functioning and recovery of the economy. To make up for missing childcare, many parents took time off from their jobs during the crisis, which reduced economic activity and tax income. Even after losing their jobs or being laid off, parents continue to pay for childcare since it may be difficult to re-enrol kids when there are few openings and extensive waitlists. This is because daycare gives parents time to hunt for new employment.

Online tutoring and education are both accessible from any location at any time. Online tutoring and learning may fill in the gaps created by a recession as it affects employment, education, money, and schedules. Particularly for colleges and other higher education institutions, online learning may be less costly than traditional classroom instruction. During the early stages of the epidemic, it also replaced many students' previous learning methods at all levels of education, from kindergarten to graduate school. Even after being permitted to return to in-person programs, many families have chosen to continue with online tutoring or classes. Additionally, online education may assist people to fill skills gaps if they are changing employment after being laid off.

Accounting and financial services

Financial and accounting services come close to being

recession-proof, yet no business or profession is completely immune. A recession is the best catalyst for individuals to think more about money. Both businesses and people want to make sure that they are utilizing their money as effectively as they can while safeguarding their future financial success. Services like CPAs, accounting, and financial planning are always in demand, regardless of the state of the economy.

Tax preparation: Both businesses and individuals will still need assistance in completing and filing their tax returns to the IRS. Additionally, they'll want to reduce their debt, thus choosing a professional provider is essential.

Accounting: During recessions, the unemployment rate for CPAs is substantially lower than the national average. When tough economic times strike, businesses rely on accountants to determine the best financial solutions. Many in the sector believe that as AI develops, it will continue to make them even more accurate and productive, increasing their demand regardless of the state of the economy.

Bookkeeping is a specialized skill that frequently determines the success or failure of a company. In a downturn, businesses need to keep meticulous financial records to maximize profits and cut costs. Because they frequently collaborate with accounting and tax preparation teams, bookkeepers are useful in both good and bad economic times.

Financial planning: When a recession hits, people are

forced to examine their past financial transgressions and consider their plans for the future, including potential recessions. Financial advisers are more in demand when the economy is struggling because people want to safeguard their wealth and make sure they'll have enough money for retirement.

Janitorial services

While commercial cleaning services may sometimes be curtailed during economic downturns, household cleaning may suffer. Cleaning is still necessary, often to specific standards, for medical offices, schools, childcare centres, retail locations, and other crucial services. If on-site custodial personnel are fired and replaced with a less costly third-party service during a recession, commercial cleaning businesses could see an increase in services.

Retail treatment

Spending decreases when times are tough financially. Many customers still want the stress-relieving benefits of retail therapy, however. Banks and food stores are replaced with pawnshops and bargain shops for loans and necessities, respectively. Luxury products, particularly those with a reputation for excellence and timelessness, are still on the minds of wealthy buyers who are unaffected by a recession.

Pawnshops: During recessions, many customers turn to pawnshops as a fallback option for modest loans when more traditional sources of credit may not be readily accessible.

Bargain retailers: As unemployment rises during recessions, spending at dollar shops and other discount retailers rises. Target and Walmart are avoided by those seeking further price cuts to stretch their budgets further. However, when recessions end and consumers start to make more money, they continue their inexpensive purchasing habits. "The same customers continued to shop for deals by choosing a tiny bottle of detergent from a dollar store rather than a larger jug at Walmart,

Luxury retail: For those who can afford it, to begin with, investing in pricey items intended for long-term use doesn't end. Luxury brands are protected by consumers who are less impacted by economic downturns and can maintain their purchasing patterns. Additionally, people tend to associate greater prices with better quality.

IT assistance

In a recession, technology use doesn't decline much. IT specialists were even more in demand during the COVID-19 recession as businesses had to find solutions and evaluate technology for work-from-home and remote-office models. Businesses want to prevent production halting due to significant technological challenges during an already stressful financial period. With IT help, everyone can operate as efficiently as possible without being hampered by technology.

Memorial services

Professionals are called in to take care of the remains and get them ready for burial or cremation when a family member dies away at home, in the hospital, or at a senior living facility. Funeral directors and staff will still be in demand even in difficult economic times, even though families may choose cheaper funeral services, caskets, and cremations during a recession.

Staffing firms

While many workers are being let off, it may seem odd that staffing companies can survive a recession. However, businesses often need to replace labour lost to layoffs with less costly alternatives. When companies still need labour but can't afford full-time employees, staffing services that provide contractors and temp workers as well as those that cover employee benefits (so a company doesn't have to) will be more in demand.

Services for digital marketing

Companies who maintained or grew their digital marketing spending continued to perform successfully, or at the very least, remained open through difficult times, as the COVID-19 recession showed. Businesses must contact customers where they are, whether via email, SEO, PPC, or social media. Companies investing in digital marketing services, particularly from agencies as opposed to employing internally, not only because they saw results but also because it is an easily trackable kind of advertising or marketing, so businesses can determine what is effective and how to increase their ROI.

Characteristics of Recession proof businesses

Recession-proof businesses have specific traits that enable them to survive challenging economic times.

There is more to it than simply persevering and hoping your fingers. Numerous firms provide specialized types of products and services that consumers and businesses still require, even in difficult economic times. Others may be adaptable and change course to weather an economic slump.

Sells necessities

Even when times are rough financially, companies that offer necessities like food, healthcare, daycare, diapers, clothing, and the like are still needed. Although customers could search for less-priced options, they will ultimately or routinely need to buy these things. Clothes will be outgrown by kids. There will be dinner cooked. Additionally, medical visits will be planned. A firm has a better chance of surviving or even thriving during a recession if it offers essential goods and services.

Offers critical maintenance services

When times are rough financially, a lot of customers and organizations want to avoid having to purchase new. You may be able to delay buying a new automobile by keeping your current one in good condition. A trip to the appliance shop could be avoided or postponed by fixing your refrigerator. When things are bad, it is simpler to spend a little money on fixing the problem rather than making a monthly payment. Businesses that provide these repair and routine maintenance services may have a smaller decline in business during a recession than other businesses.

Manages financial flow effectively

Even if your company doesn't fit any of the

aforementioned categories, you can still adapt if you know how to manage cash flow during difficult times. Requesting shorter payment terms from consumers, for instance, and beginning to increase your cash on hand right away.

Serves clients who are untouched by economic downturns

Serving the sorts of consumers who are unaffected by fluctuations in the financial markets is one strategy for surviving a recession. Those who are already rich or used to purchasing upscale goods often will keep doing so. Additionally, clients may move to more expensive brands with a good reputation for quality since they know the product will last. Although inflation and recessions don't always go hand in hand, demand may increase since luxury products often keep their worth during this time. Additionally, B2B companies that work with these recession-resistant companies won't see a significant decline in accounts receivable.

Sells unique things that cannot be found elsewhere.

There are no other companies out there attempting to undercut you on pricing for specialized or trademarked items with little competition. Being in a "blue ocean" provides advantages at all times, but in a downturn, it is advantageous since your company is the only one providing a niche product or service. Serving a specialized market has its advantages, too.

Dispenses required products or services

Regardless of economic conditions, there will always be a need for goods or services that are mandated by the law or by certain organizations. For example, states mandate automobile insurance for people and companies who need mobility. Businesses must invest in new equipment and maintain it regularly to comply with permits and safety rules. Businesses or organizations that provide goods or services in line with these requirements often see little change during economic downturns.

Ability to adapt to the times

Agility and flexibility are essential for every organization to survive a downturn, regardless of the goods or services it offers.

To swiftly adapt to changing conditions, plans and tactics must be adjusted. For instance, after being forced to shut their indoor dining rooms due to lockdowns, restaurants immediately changed course during the COVID-19 recession to provide online ordering as well as no-contact delivery and pick up. Some hotels began providing day rates for work-from-home workers who wished to leave the house after being severely impacted by the slowdown in travel. Additionally, distilleries halted producing alcohol and rushed to produce hand sanitiser as soon as they learned about the pandemic supply chain problems. The ability to change course and adapt to the situation at hand may make the difference between surviving and flourishing under trying circumstances.

Although not every company can be recession-proof or countercyclical, businesses may nevertheless safeguard themselves by planning for potential situations and how they might adjust. Businesses may re-engage their core consumers for repeat business, prepare for the worst, and even engage money in advance to have access to cash when they need it in addition to being nimble and conserving capital. The issue is not whether but rather when will the next recession occur. Your firm can remain open and successful if you start preparing now.

FAQs about the Recession-Proof Business Model

How can a company survive a downturn?

Businesses that are recession-proof consistently bring in money, regardless of how the economy is doing. In times of economic difficulty, these businesses may adapt to meet the changing demands of their target clients or focus on specialized markets to guarantee that they are the only ones catering to that demographic. Being required by your clients, regardless of how the economy is doing, is the key to being recession-proof.

How can a company cut costs during a recession?

Managing firm cash flows and reining down expenditure are the greatest ways to conserve during a recession. To achieve this, you may have to give customers shorter payment terms, provide rewards for paying early, and manage your vendor connections to get longer payment terms. Other methods for saving money when business resources are tight include reducing overhead and minimizing waste. Finally, when revenue fails, some companies do ultimately have to turn to layoffs and other cost-cutting measures.

How do small firms fare during a recession?

Due to their efforts to cut costs and avoid waste, consumers may make fewer purchases or pay bills later during a recession. Both this decline in demand and the delay in payments have a significant negative impact on small firms. Budget cutbacks result in personnel layoffs and restrictions on marketing. Smaller firms often struggle to get credit, making it more challenging to use loans to solve these cash flow problems.

CHAPTER 5

BUILDING YOUR WEALTH

Even though it may seem paradoxical to some, you may still accumulate money during a recession. According to experts, a recession may be one of the ideal periods to increase your wealth. How can one achieve it precisely?

Certificate of Deposit

Frequently, you just need $500 to establish a certificate of deposit (CD). You'll start earning interest on your money as a result. But there are other advantages to opening a CD as well. I typically prefer to put money in six-month CDs, and every six months I combine everything that I've earned and start a new CD that has a greater interest rate. This stops me from ever accessing my money, which is why I enjoy CDs in the first place. Find CDs with the greatest interest rate offers by using Bankrate. Your ZIP code may be used to modify the location. The website also allows you to choose the deposit quantities and the length of the CD, and it provides a list of nearby banks and credit unions.

Learn to Invest in Technology

Robo-advisers, such as Betterment and Wealthfront, provide low-cost investment management that automates investment selection and even the monthly portfolio rebalancing procedure necessary to create a reliable investment portfolio as a novice. Investing allows you to earn compound returns on your money, which over time will enable you to double or even treble your savings. The greatest time to start investing is during a recession since you may purchase stocks at a lower price and then sell them when the market recovers. Look for a fee-only, fiduciary financial advisor that would charge you for a brief, hourly engagement to help you get started on the proper track if you're unsure where to invest.

Find Stocks That Have Been Significantly Discounted

Emotion often drives short-term stock market choices, and recessions lead to a lot of emotional decision-making, according to F. For long-term investors, recessions are excellent times to increase the number of shares they own in their portfolios because when sellers panic and liquidate, the price of equities falls for purchasers. If you typically spend $100 on 10 shares, a 30% stock market decrease implies you may now spend that same $100 on 14 shares.

Order Silver

Buying precious metals like silver is another smart strategy to increase your wealth during a downturn. In contrast, if you hold an asset like a stock, bond, or mutual fund and that firm goes bankrupt, which occurs regularly during recessions, you are left with nothing. Silver is inexpensive in comparison to gold, and once you possess it, no one can take it away from you. Before purchasing, do thorough research on precious metals merchants and ensure that the 0.9999 pure silver bullion rounds or bars are near to the "spot price," or current pricing.

Get Gold

History has shown that when economic downturns happen, the majority of economies and investors turn to gold as a haven for preserving their wealth, Therefore, the precious metal becomes scarce, leading to massive gains in value. Buying gold at the beginning of a recession is another sure way to grow wealth as a recession deepens. In terms of buying gold, time is important. Only acquire gold during the first phases of a recession or other major financial crisis. For example, those of us who are familiar with gold bought it when COVID-19 was proclaimed a worldwide pandemic. According to what we know, the price of metal is at an all-time high right now.

Use the Dollar-Cost Averaging Method When Investing

A long-term investment strategy known as dollar-cost averaging involves investing a specific sum of money in the same stock or fund regularly, such as once a month. It is a method of investing that enables you to acquire assets over a certain length of time using a set sum of money. This method enables you to buy more shares when the price is low and fewer shares when the price is high since the amount of money you spend each month remains the same. With this strategy, you may participate in various share prices across numerous investment cycles. Finally, you may do away with the need to time the market by consistently investing and using dollar cost averaging.

Keep Your Company's 401(k) Program in Mind

A recession is a favourable moment to start investing since it presents a chance to purchase at a discount, by the opinions of many other financial advisors. Making an investment in your company's 401(k), which doesn't need a minimum amount of money to start, is another method to take advantage of the situation. Start investing in your 401(k) if your employer matches your contributions, since this is a very wise move. The employer's match will give you an instant 100% return on your investment. In addition, because your contributions will lower your taxable income, you will pay less tax to the IRS at the end of the year.

Create Streams of Passive Income

Having an 8 a.m. to 5 p.m. job means you may be cut off from your income at the least disturbance of your work life. However, if you create a passive income stream, you may continue to amass money even during a recession. The "physical economy" is unlikely to affect your passive streams. Selling online stock photos, purchasing equities, and affiliate marketing are just a few of the profitable passive income alternatives offered. Affiliate marketing sometimes referred to as affiliate advertising, is the practice of generating commissions by endorsing the goods or services of other people's companies.

Purchase Real estate

Recessions are when most real estate wealth is created. I would search for a modest investment property, such as a duplex with decent bones but a distressed seller if I was just starting and had some money to invest. It's a good idea to network with local realtors that specialize in this field. You want something that's near a government or university campus, excellent, solid blue-collar employment, and where most of the fixing up can be done with sweat equity.

Take Advantage of Low-Interest Rates

Recessions may be advantageous for company expansion since financing rates are often at record lows. Banks will cut their rates to unthinkable levels during recessions because of the low demand for loans from the general population; take advantage of this and invest the money in something that will provide a higher return than the rate (interest). This will immediately become a reliable source of revenue.

Consider Yourself a Business

The things you spend money on must be profitable or cost you less elsewhere.

It's a good idea to review your recent purchases, evaluate your spending patterns, and determine the worth of the things you're spending money on. For instance, if you buy a house, you may save money in addition to the real estate gains you'll receive vs renting.

Online Auctions for Unwanted Items

Selling your old items online might earn you money.

Consider the items in your workplace or house that are not in use. "This might be jewellery, technology, apparel, or furnishings. You may monetize your used items on a variety of websites, including eBay, Tradesy, and RealReal.

Rent out a Room

Does your house have additional room? Think about renting out a room to get passive income: "During the recession, you may rent out a room to make additional money. It will assist in generating more income and cut down on tax and utility bill expenses.

Mortgage Refinancing

Refinancing your home or other debt that you may be paying interest on might be a great option during a recession. By doing this, you may reduce your expenses and charges. " Finding methods to pay off debt or cut interest is one of the finest strategies to generate wealth, particularly during a recession, since it has been shown that doing so offers one of the highest returns on your investment.

Take Advantage of Chances to Reduce Costs

You should concentrate on areas where you can reduce expenses and save money if you want to develop wealth during a recession. Fortunately, a recession provides many opportunities for substantial savings, which may help you amass significant wealth. For instance, a lot of companies are discounting and reducing the prices of their goods and services. Take advantage of these kinds of offers now as a customer to save money.

Reduce Your Debt

You must control your debt if you want to accumulate riches. Being heavily indebted will make it difficult for you to accumulate wealth and will cost you money because of interest charges. "Some loans are acceptable since they enable you to accumulate money, like real estate. However, if you're having trouble paying off loans or credit card debt, make a strategy to do so. When striving to reduce debt and accumulate money, it's essential to consider how destructive compound interest may be. If you merely make the bare minimum payments each month, the interest alone may cause your debt to increase. Pay as much as you can toward high-interest debt each month to break the endless cycle.

Develop and Sustain Business Connections

That opportunity will present itself to those who seek it is perhaps one of the most important truths to keep in mind, especially during a recession. Maintaining connections with business contacts who may be able to put you in touch with employment or other vital chances to make money might be more crucial than ever at a time when opportunities may be harder to come by. In business friendships, you must take the initiative rather than wait for things to happen. When you haven't talked to a buddy in a while, it's simple to get in touch with them again, but doing business is another story. When you spend time away from other business experts, it may be possible for someone in your industry or line of work to infiltrate your market. If this happens, who will your ally recommend when a business opportunity arises? Their brand-new closest pal.

Invest in Yourself

If you've lost your job, it might be a good idea to... perhaps take a class to gain another credential for your resume, or even consider going back to school to earn a degree. "I used the 2008-2009 recession as motivation to get my master's degree, and it permanently increased my employability and earning power," says one person who invested in themselves during a recession.

www.ingramcontent.com/pod-product-compliance
Lightning Source LLC
LaVergne TN
LVHW050346160826
845677LV00014B/3813